GRAYSCALE
COLORING BOOK

WONDERFUL
BEAUTIFUL
BUTTERFLIES
ADULT
COLORING BOOK

VOLUME 2.

PATTERNS FOR RELAXATION AND STRESS RELIEF

COLOR TEST PAGE

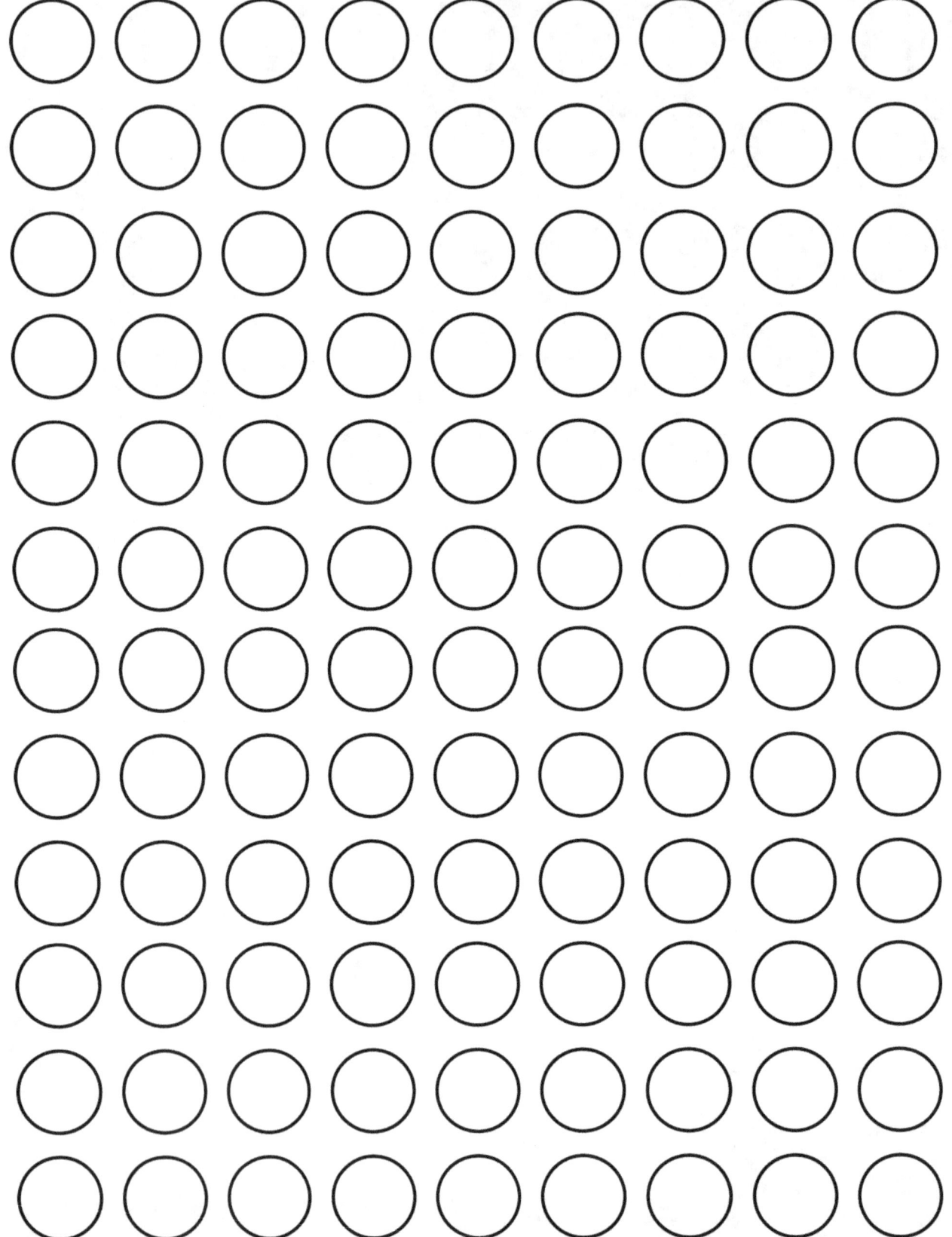

COLOR TEST PAGE

www.ingramcontent.com/pod-product-compliance
Lightning Source LLC
Chambersburg PA
CBHW080548190526
45169CB00007B/2682